CONTENTS

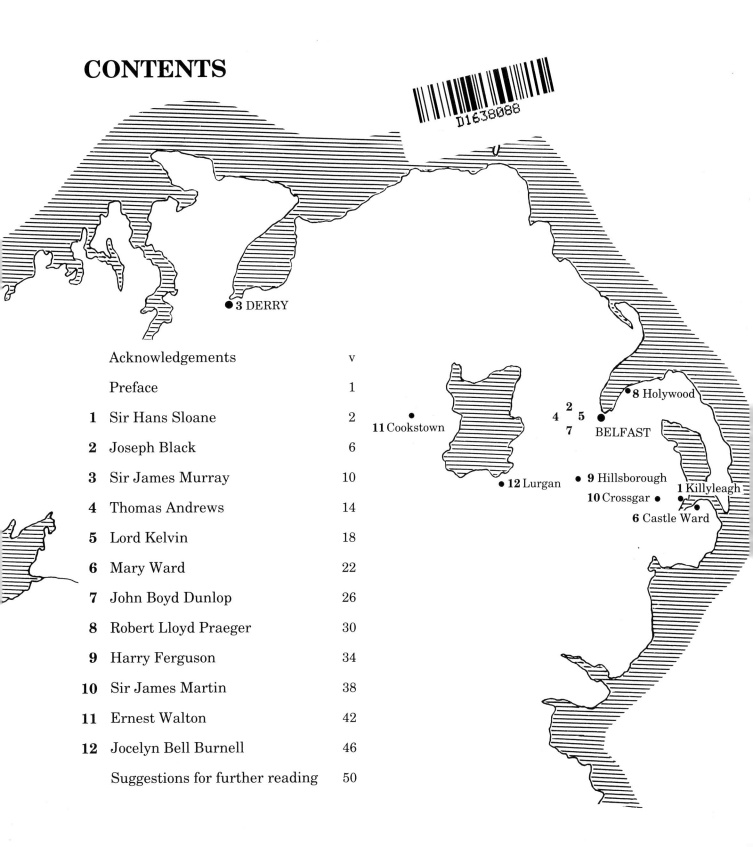

3 DERRY

Acknowledgements		v
Preface		1
1	Sir Hans Sloane	2
2	Joseph Black	6
3	Sir James Murray	10
4	Thomas Andrews	14
5	Lord Kelvin	18
6	Mary Ward	22
7	John Boyd Dunlop	26
8	Robert Lloyd Praeger	30
9	Harry Ferguson	34
10	Sir James Martin	38
11	Ernest Walton	42
12	Jocelyn Bell Burnell	46
	Suggestions for further reading	50

2 **8** Holywood

4 **5**

7 BELFAST

11 Cookstown

9 Hillsborough

12 Lurgan

10 Crossgar

1 Killyleagh

6 Castle Ward

D1638088

ACKNOWLEDGEMENTS

We would like to take this opportunity to thank all those who helped us in the search for appropriate information.

To the staff of the following: Belfast Central Library; the Linen Hall Library, Belfast; the Reference Library, Ballymena; the Science Library, Queen's University Belfast; the Ulster Folk and Transport Museum; and the Ulster Museum.

To the following individuals: Professor D. Thorburn Burns (School of Chemistry) and Dr Owen Harry (School of Biology and Biochemistry), Queen's University Belfast; Professor Jocelyn Bell Burnell and Professor Ernest Walton; W.A.L. Alford, Mary Campbell, Trevor Gray and James Martin; Alistair Edwards and Ken Pee. Also a special thanks to all those who provided us with useful hints and snippets of relevant information.

Our thanks are also due to the following for allowing us to reproduce illustrations: the Royal Society, London (pp. 2, 18); Professor D. Thorburn Burns (p. 7, bottom); the National Trust in Northern Ireland (pp. 22, 23, 24, 25); the Ulster Museum (pp. 26, 29 top, 31); the Ulster Folk and Transport Museum (pp. 27, 34, 35, 38); Allen Figgis and Company (pp. 30, 31, 32); the Ford Motor Company (p. 37, top and bottom); the Martin-Baker Company (p. 39, top); National Portrait Gallery, London (p. 42); P. Paice (p. 45, top and bottom); Professor Jocelyn Bell Burnell (p. 46).

Finally we would particularly like to thank the Northern Ireland Education Support Unit of the School of Education at Queen's University Belfast, BP Oil UK Limited and the Blackstaff Press, without whom this concept would not have become reality.

Sponsored by BP Oil

PREFACE

There is an overall lack of awareness of the major role played by many people from Northern Ireland who have made significant contributions to science and technology. This may be due in part to a dearth of suitable information in a readily available form, to a parochial undervaluing of local talent and enterprise, or to the fact that scientists tend to communicate with one another in a language that is often incomprehensible to the general reader.

We have attempted to redress this situation by gathering together pen portraits on twelve of these remarkable men and women. Where possible, we have tried to investigate their early education, how they became interested in their specific fields, and the impact their discoveries and inventions made on the wider world. The task of deciding who to include was not an easy one, but we have endeavoured to span the last three centuries and to cover all the sciences and technology.

The educational system has undergone vast changes with the introduction of the Northern Ireland Curriculum. Not only are there new areas of science, but there are also cross-curricular themes, which have proved challenging to science teachers, not least in the teaching of a programme of study to all pupils from five to sixteen years of age. *Northern Ireland Scientists and Inventors* will be a useful resource for schoolchildren, helping them to learn about local scientists and technologists, for too often we tend to look further afield for instances of brilliant discoveries and inventions, not realising that there are appropriate examples from our own region. This publication will be especially helpful to those considering how to incorporate the cross-curricular themes of Cultural Heritage and Education for Mutual Understanding into science courses and will be relevant to other areas of the curriculum, like history and geography. The book will also appeal to Northern Ireland people generally, at home and abroad, and particularly so to those with an interest in local history.

WILBERT GARVIN AND DES O'RAWE
BELFAST, NOVEMBER 1992

Sir Hans Sloane, 1716

Places of residence

Killyleagh, County Down 1660–79
Water Lane, London 1679–83
France 1683–4
London 1684–7
West Indies 1687–9
London 1689–95
4 Bloomsbury Place, London 1695–1712
Chelsea, London 1712–53

Family

Father   Alexander Sloane
Mother   Sarah Hickes
Married   Elizabeth Rose, 1695
Children One son and three daughters

Hans Sloane was born on 16 April 1660 at **Killyleagh** in County Down, the youngest in a family of seven sons. His father – who died when Hans was only six – was a man of considerable standing and property, being the Receiver-General of Taxes; he had come from Scotland with James Hamilton during the reign of James I.

Hamilton provided education for the children of his followers, so Killyleagh became an important centre of learning – it even had a school of philosophy founded by the Hamilton family. Hans was educated locally and as a young boy he often visited the excellent library in Killyleagh Castle.

From an early age he was keenly interested in natural history; County Down and Strangford Lough have always been ideal places for such study. He wrote: *'I had from my youth been very much pleas'd with the Study of Plants, and other Parts of Nature, and had seen most of those Kinds of Curiosities, which are to be found either in the Fields, or in the Gardens or Cabinets of the Curious in these Parts.'* He visited the Copeland Islands, off the County Down coast, and was impressed by the number of sea birds there. He also noted that the local people chewed dulse as a remedy for scurvy.

Hans became very ill when he was 16; he possibly suffered an attack of tuberculosis, since he was coughing blood. At that time such a disease was usually fatal, but he survived, as he described, *'by temperance, and abstaining from wine, and other fermented liquors, and the prudent management of myself in all other respects'*. He probably also had smallpox, for his face is pockmarked in later portrait paintings.

Physician & Naturalist

Hans had recovered well enough by the time he was 19 to go to London to study anatomy and medicine. He also took classes in chemistry and was influenced by Robert Boyle, another Irishman and the father of modern chemistry. His interest in botany continued and he became friendly with the well-known botanist, John Ray.

In 1683 Hans set off to Europe to further his education. He attended botany and anatomy lectures in Paris and Montpellier, but, being a Protestant, he was unable to take a degree in these places. However, he graduated as a Doctor of Physick (medicine) from the Huguenot University of Orange, near Avignon. Due to religious persecution, he returned to London in 1684 to practise medicine, and on 21 January the following year he was elected a fellow of the Royal Society, which had recently been established by Charles II. On Boyle's recommendation he was admitted as a fellow of the Royal College of Physicians on 12 April 1687.

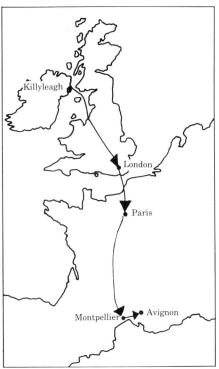

Sloane's educational travels

On 12 September 1687 Sloane went to Jamaica as physician to the 2nd Duke of Albemarle, who had been appointed governor there, and he also acted as surgeon to the West Indies fleet. He was fascinated by the wide variety of flora and fauna there. He collected 800 new plant specimens and published a catalogue of them in Latin in 1696. He wrote a book about his travels – *Voyage to Madeira, Barbadoes, and Jamaica; with the Natural History of Jamaica* – which appeared in two volumes in 1707 and 1725 and described the voyage and his observations on the inhabitants, diseases, plants, animals, climate and so on.

In 1689 Sloane returned to England to find that William III had replaced James II on the throne. He married Elizabeth Rose, a widow, on 11 May 1695 and lived in London, where

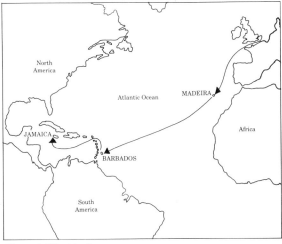

Sloane's West Indies voyage

Sir Hans Sloane

Article from the *Philosophical Transactions of the Royal Society,* 1722

On one occasion when Handel was visiting, he caused Sloane considerable distress by placing a hot buttered muffin on one of his precious books.

he practised medicine. His fee for the rich was one guinea (a gold coin worth one pound and one shilling) an hour, but he rose early and every morning, until ten o'clock, he treated the poor for free. His fees, his investments in quinine bark and sugar, not to mention his wife's fortune, made him a very wealthy man. He became acquainted with the most learned people of society, listing among his friends Newton, Liebnitz, Linnaeus, Halley, Locke, Pepys, Evelyn, Pope and Handel. In 1712 he bought a country house in Chelsea and set up the famous Physick Gardens there; that same year he was appointed physician to Queen Anne.

Hans Sloane was knighted by George I on 3 April 1716, and on 30 September 1719 he was elected president of the Royal College of Physicians in London. He published the fourth *London Pharmacopoeia,* which contained a catalogue of medicinal herbs, clear definitions of their properties and how they could be identified. In a volume of the *Philosophical Transactions of the Royal Society,* edited by him, he stressed the difference between '*Matters of Fact, Experiment, or Observation, and what is called Hypothesis'.*

Sir Hans was a health fanatic, probably as a result of his illnesses when he was young. He lived his life by the dictum '*Sobriety, temperance and moderation are the best and most powerful preservatives that Nature has granted to Mankind.'* He believed that diet played an essential role in good health. When he was in Jamaica he had seen babies fed on cocoa beans and no other food than their mothers' milk; so he decided to produce a health drink for children at home by mixing chocolate with cows' milk. The result was known as Sir Hans Sloane's Milk Chocolate, a recipe that was used by Cadbury's until 1885.

He advised the Royal Navy on how to keep ships' crews healthy and free from **deficiency diseases** such as scurvy, and played an important part in establishing the practice of **immunisation** against smallpox, introduced in 1718. He inoculated members of the royal family.

In 1727 the president of the Royal Society, Sir Isaac Newton, died, and Sloane was elected to succeed him, a post he held until 1741; he was, therefore, the only person ever to jointly preside over the Royal Society and the Royal College of Physicians. The same year he was appointed physician to George II.

Sir Hans died on 11 January 1753 after an illness of only three days, so despite his poor health in early life he survived to the ripe old age of 92. In his will his magnificent collections of specimens, books (over 50,000) and manuscripts (3,500 bound volumes) were offered to the nation for a sum of £20,000, to be paid to his surviving daughters. These formed the nucleus around which the vast collections of the **British Museum** have grown. Sloane Square, Sloane Street, Hans Place and Hans Road in London perpetuate his memory.

The **Hans Sloane Memorial Fund** was set up in the early 1960s. Each year awards of money are given to the three candidates with the highest marks in the combined Northern Ireland A level examinations in biology, chemistry and physics; the first prizewinner is also presented with the **Hans Sloane Medal**.

There are two plaques commemorating Sir Hans in Killyleagh. One, fixed to a large rock taken from Strangford Lough, can be seen at the entrance to the castle, and the other is at the site of his birthplace.

Cadbury's label

The British Museum, opened in 1759

The Hans Sloane Medal, struck in bronze by the trustees of the British Museum in 1953

2 Joseph Black

1728–1799

An engraving of Joseph Black

Places of residence

Bordeaux, France 1728–40
Belfast 1740–6
Glasgow 1746–51
Edinburgh 1751–6
Glasgow 1756–66
Edinburgh 1766–99

Family

Father   John Black
Mother   Margaret Gordon

Joseph Black was born in Bordeaux, France, on 16 April 1728. His father, John Black, a wine merchant from **Belfast**, had married Margaret Gordon, the daughter of an Aberdeen man living in Bordeaux. The Black family had settled in Ulster during the plantation of James I, and was originally called Macgillie Dhu (son of the black servant). Joseph's grandfather, John Black, was a burgess of the town of Belfast and his great-uncle, Sir John Eccles, had been lord mayor of Dublin. The Black family was very friendly with Captain John McCracken, the father of United Irishman Henry Joy and his sister Mary Ann.

Young Joseph was educated at home by his mother, who taught all her 13 children to read and write English. When he was 12 he was sent to live with his Belfast relations, and he became a pupil of the old Latin School there, where he learned the three Rs, Greek and Latin. The school, established by the Earl of Donegall in 1666, stood on the corner of Ann Street and Church Lane, which was then called School-house Lane. It remained in existence until the Belfast Academy was established in Academy Street in 1786.

Since no university then existed in Ulster, Joseph was sent to Glasgow University when he was 18. For three years he studied languages and natural philosophy (the old name for physics). The college album of 1746 refers to him, typically in Latin in those days: *Josephus Black filius natu quartus Joannis Black Mercatoris in Urbe Bordeaux in Gallia, ex urbe de Belfast in Hibernia.*

Pressed by his father to choose a profession, he decided to study medicine and attended the chemistry lectures of Dr William Cullen, who was the first to teach this subject in Glasgow University. Up until about this time chemistry had been treated only as a *'curious, and in some respects, a useless art practised by reprobates'*. Cullen, recognising young Black's keenness, employed him as a laboratory assistant, and supported him in his studies.

After a further three years at Glasgow, Joseph went to Edinburgh University to finish his education in medicine, and in 1754 he received his degree. His thesis – *'De humore acido a cibis orto, et magnesia alba'* – proved to be a classic work in chemistry.

In 1756, before the Philosophical Society of Edinburgh, Black described in detail his experiments and the conclusions he deduced from them. He reported that the compound we now call calcium carbonate was converted to calcium oxide when heated strongly, giving off a gas which would recombine with the calcium oxide to form calcium carbonate again. Black called this gas **fixed air** because it could be fixed into a solid form again. We now call it **carbon dioxide**.

At that time gases were regarded as mysterious, or even spiritual bodies. In fact Jean Baptiste van Helmont (1577–1644) coined the term 'gas' from the Greek *chaos*, meaning space, for the 'wild and untameable spirits' which could not be condensed. By involving a gas in a chemical reaction, Black showed that it is not very different from liquids or solids. Since the calcium oxide was reconverted into calcium carbonate by exposure to air, it showed that carbon dioxide was part of our atmosphere. Black also showed that carbon dioxide acts like an acid and that it is produced during fermentation, respiration and the combustion of carbon.

Black used the chemical balance more systematically in

Glasgow University in the 18th century

DISSERTATIO MEDICA
INAUGURALIS,

D E

HUMORE ACIDO

A CIBIS ORTO,

E T

MAGNESIA ALBA:

QUAM,

ANNUENTE SUMMO NUMINE,

Ex Auctoritate Reverendi admodum Viri

D. JOANNIS GOWDIE,

ACADEMIAE EDINBURGENAE PRAEFECTI,

NEC NON

Amplissimi SENATUS ACADEMICI consensu,

Et nobilissimae FACULTATIS MEDICAE decreto,

PRO GRADU DOCTORATUS,

SUMMISQUE IN MEDICINA HONORIBUS ET PRIVILEGIIS
RITE ET LEGITIME CONSEQUENDIS,
ERUDITORUM EXAMINI SUBJICIT

JOSEPHUS BLACK Gallus.

Ad diem 11 Junii, horâ locoque solitis.

EDINBURGI:

Apud G. Hamilton et J. Balfour.

ACADEMIAE TYPOGRAPHOS,

MDCCLIV.

Title page of Joseph Black's MD thesis

Joseph Black

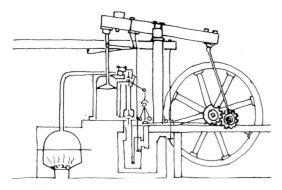

Watt's steam engine

James Watt's use of Black's principles in developing the steam engine is a good example of scientific theory leading technology; conversely, the germ of Black's idea may have been obtained from a Scottish distiller friend.

his work than any other chemist had done before him, and performed a series of experiments with all the accuracy he could command. His technique of chemical measurement was to come into its own a few decades later in the methods of Antoine Lavoisier. It was Lavoisier who recommended that Black be appointed one of the eight foreign associates of the Académie Royale des Sciences in Paris.

When he was 28 Joseph became professor of chemistry at Glasgow University, where he remained until 1766. During this period he ran a demanding medical practice and his eager and curious mind also unearthed two more fundamental discoveries – **latent heat** and **specific heat**. He was the first to recognise the difference between **quantity** of heat and its **intensity**, which we now call **temperature**. Black found that when ice was heated it did not rise in temperature until it had melted. He concluded that the heat absorbed must be hidden or **latent**. A similar occurrence took place when water became steam. He also showed that equal masses of different substances required **different** quantities of heat to increase in temperature by a fixed amount. We now call this quantity **specific heat**.

James Watt, a laboratory assistant at Glasgow University, realised that an early version of the steam engine was very inefficient. He discussed the problem with Joseph Black, who explained to him his theory of latent heat. The solution suddenly came to Watt on his way home and he went on to invent the first successful steam engine. Black lent him a large sum of money to develop this invention, which gave an enormous impetus to the Industrial Revolution.

After Henry Cavendish discovered hydrogen in 1766, Black suggested that it could be used in blowing up light bladders (balloons) to make them float in the air.

Joseph Black

In 1776 Joseph Black became professor of chemistry at Edinburgh University. His reputation as a lecturer was such that men from Germany, Switzerland, Scandinavia and even Russia and America attended his classes. His lectures were so clear that they could be easily understood by people with little or no scientific background. Not only were his students instructed, but they were also entertained. Daniel Rutherford, the discoverer of nitrogen, and the renowned physicist Thomas Young, who discovered the wave theory of light, were listed among his students.

Black never married but he had a large circle of friends whom he met regularly at dining clubs in Edinburgh. His closest friends were Adam Smith, author of the famous book *The Wealth of Nations*, published in 1776, and James Hutton, the father of geology, whose *Theory of the Earth* first appeared in 1785. Many others, including the philosopher David Hume, formed what became known as the Scottish Enlightenment.

Black had many talents: he produced fine artwork in figures and landscape, had a keen musical ear and was an excellent judge of musical compositions. He amassed a fortune of £20,000 by careful financial management, and his biographers have stated that he made many loans to his friends and treated poor patients without charge.

Joseph Black was never a healthy man; he managed to conserve his strength by careful diet and moderate exercise. He dreaded a prolonged illness because he did not wish to inflict trouble and distress on his close friends. In the 71st year of his life his health failed him and on 26 November 1799 he died peacefully at his home in Edinburgh.

Henry Cockburn, one of Black's students, gave the following description of him in his later years:

'He was a striking and beautiful person; tall, very thin, and cadaverously pale; his hair carefully powdered, though there was little of it except what was collected in a long thin queue; his eyes dark, clear and large like deep pools of pure water. He wore black speckless clothes, silk stockings, silver buckles, and either a slim green silk umbrella, or a genteel brown cane. The general frame and air were feeble and slender. The wildest boy respected Black. No lad could be irreverent toward a man so pale, so gentle, so elegant and so illustrious. So he glided, like a spirit, through our rather mischievous sportiveness,unharmed.'

'I may say, to him I owe in great measure my being what I am; he taught me to reason and experiment in natural philosophy, and was always a true friend and adviser, whose loss will always be lamented while I live.'

James Watt, 16 December 1799, on hearing of Black's death

3 Sir James Murray   1788–1871

Sir James Murray in his 60s

Places of residence

Derry 1788–1804
Edinburgh 1804–7
Dublin 1807–8
Belfast 1808–31
Dublin 1831–71

Family

Father   Edward Murray
Mother   Not known
Married   H. Sharrock, 1809
Children   Two sons

James Murray was born in **Derry** in 1788, the eldest son of Edward Murray. He set out on a medical career, completing his studies at the College of Surgeons in Edinburgh in 1807; he then went to Dublin and became a member of the College of Surgeons there.

In 1808 he set up a practice in Belfast, where he went on to have a distinguished career. During this time he carried out research on a wide range of projects.

In 1812 he devised a way of making solid magnesia into a liquid form: he dissolved magnesium carbonate in water through which carbon dioxide had been bubbled. Milk of magnesia is, of course, still taken today as a laxative and as a cure for stomach pains.

Such a discovery, together with his well-known medical talents, brought him wealth and reputation, and introduced him, while he was still a young man, to the notice of important people. In 1817 he published a paper entitled 'Danger of using solid magnesia, and on its great value in a fluid state for internal use'. He patented his process and set up a commercial manufacturing plant in Belfast.

In the course of the production process at Murray's chemical works silicates and bicarbonate of soda and potash were building up in heaps as waste. He already knew, from experiments conducted near Belfast in 1808, that bones treated with sulphuric acid produced biphosphate of lime and that when this was added to the soil, it improved crop growth. He thought that his waste chemicals could be used for this purpose. His first trials were carried out in 1817, when the waste chemicals were spread on pasture lands in the Point Fields, near York Street in Belfast. The chemicals were mixed with composts, rough phosphates and a small amount of ordinary manure. For several years, apparently, the fields provided excellent grazing land for a large number of cows which produced good-quality milk.

In 1831 Murray was appointed resident physician to the lord lieutenant of Ireland, the Marquis of Anglesey, and he was also knighted. He moved to Dublin and over the next 10 years he served three lord lieutenants.

In 1835 he delivered a series of lectures, at the Royal Exchange in Dublin, on the use of soluble phosphate of lime and other chemical substances as fertiliser. He was, therefore, the first person to produce **superphosphate**, although he mixed it with other imported materials like guano (the dried droppings of sea birds) and nitrate of soda to produce a compound fertiliser.

In 1841 Sir James published a booklet, *Advice to Farmers*, in which he listed three types of 'oxygenated fertiliser' for various crops. By that year he was engaged in the fertiliser business on a grand scale: *'Many manufactories are preparing at certain distances, and several steam mills are at work for crushing and grinding materials in each district.'*

On 12 May 1842 his son, John Fisher Murray, a barrister-at-law but better known as a poet and humorist, applied for a Scottish patent, followed on 23 May by an English patent. Basically, Murray reacted phosphorite of lime with sulphuric acid; the resulting paste was mixed in an earthern vessel for two or three days and then an absorbent substance was added, for example, bran, sawdust, dust of malt, husks of seeds, refuse of flax leaves, bark or dry earth. The liquid form was thus converted into a powder, which prevented loss by leakage, was safer and easier to carry and, most importantly, the chemicals were released gradually into the soil.

Advertisement in the *Northern Whig*, 31 May 1842

Sir James Murray

Summary of Murray's second 'Chemical lecture on agriculture', *Belfast Commercial Chronicle*, 1842

Meantime various experiments were being carried out on the new fertiliser to find out if it was better than ordinary manure. During 1842 trials were held in Dublin: at Terenure in the suburbs, at Aughrim Street near the North Circular Road, and at the Royal Dublin Society's Botanic Gardens.

There was some criticism of the way in which these trials were handled and, as Murray pointed out, *'experiments conducted on small plots of land and on a small scale can be apt to mislead, as their contrast is more marked than when we come to deal with the broad and unequal expanse of a farm or a field'*.

In 1842 he delivered three lectures on the subject of chemical agriculture at the Belfast Museum, which drew large attendances from the principal landlords and their families.

In 1843 he published his detailed findings in a book — *Trials and Effects of Chemical Fertilisers with Various Experiments in Agriculture*. Many people were now using Murray's artificial fertilisers, including Mr Ferguson, the curator of the Botanic Gardens in Belfast, who found that it more than doubled the growth of grass.

Despite the publicity through his publications and his lectures, Murray does not seem to have been competent enough at marketing to make his superphosphate business as prosperous as it could have been. His main competitor, John Bennet Lawes, eventually bought his patent in 1846, and built up a very successful artificial fertiliser industry.

During 1849 Sir James returned to the manufacture of fluid magnesia with one of his sons, Edward.

In 1857 he took out a second patent on fertilisers. During this year he retired from his medical duties; he was still attached to two Dublin hospitals and was Inspector of Anatomy for Ireland for nearly 40 years.

Sir James always showed concern for his fellow man, continually striving to reduce suffering and prevent disease. In 1849 he published *Electricity as a Cause of Cholera and Other Epidemics, and the Relation of Galvanism to the Action of Remedies*, in which he proposed that, in order to prevent cholera, a layer of non-conducting material be placed underneath the ground floors of houses. He also published *Heat and Humidity* and *Medical Effects of Atmospheric Pressure*.

Murray died in Dublin on Friday 8 December 1871 and there were many tributes to him and his work in the national press. The following obituary notice appeared in the *Irish Times* on 10 December 1871:

> *There was something truly liberal and dignified in his manners and his person. No-one could more effectively give a word of good advice to the young, or of encouragement to the deserving, or with a more pungent wit could rebuke the vain or arrogant. A most perfect tolerance in matters of creed and party distinguished him. He was himself a Catholic, and a supporter of what is still called the Liberal party; but his friendship and benevolence were as wide as the fraternity of man.*

4 Thomas Andrews 1813–1885

Etching based on a photograph of Thomas Andrews, taken in Paris when he was 62 years old

Places of residence

3 Donegall Square South, Belfast 1813–28
Glasgow 1828–30
Paris 1830–1
Dublin 1831–3
Edinburgh 1833–5
Belfast 1835–49
Lennoxvale, Malone Road, Belfast (presently the residence of the vice-chancellor of Queen's) 1849–79
Fortwilliam Park, Belfast 1879–85

Family

Father   Thomas John Andrews
Mother   Elizabeth Stevenson
Married Jane Hardie Walker, 1842
Children Two sons and three daughters

Thomas Andrews was born on 19 December 1813 at Donegall Square South in **Belfast**, just a short distance from Lord Kelvin's future birthplace. His father, a wealthy linen merchant at the White Linen Hall, sent young Thomas to school at the Belfast Academy in Academy Street (now BRA, which moved in 1876 to the Cliftonville Road). After a few years Thomas transferred to the Belfast Academical Institution in College Square East (now RBAI or Inst.) where he progressed well. One of his school reports described him as a *'modest, silent boy with a great capacity for general knowledge'*.

After working for a short time in his father's office, he went, when he was only 15, to study chemistry at Glasgow University, hoping to find new ways of improving the manufacture of linen. After two years there he went to Paris to continue his studies under the famous French chemist Jean Baptiste Dumas (Andrews and Louis Pasteur were his most brilliant pupils). Apparently Andrews had no difficulty following the lectures or taking notes in French, which says much for his French teacher at Inst., Monsieur Adelbert D'Oisy, who was, in fact, a Parisian, and also acted as French vice-consul to the port of Belfast. While in Paris Andrews became acquainted with Joseph Louis Gay-Lussac and Antoine César Becquerel, the foremost French scientists at that time.

On returning to Ireland, Andrews studied classics as well as medical science at Trinity College Dublin. He then decided to continue his studies at Edinburgh University, obtaining a medical degree at the age of 22, his thesis being on the circulation and properties of blood.

He finally came back to Belfast to practise medicine, and

was also appointed professor of chemistry at Inst., which at that time provided the nearest thing to a university education in the area. In 1845 he became vice-president and later the first professor of chemistry at the new Queen's College, Belfast (in 1908 it received the royal charter and became the Queen's University of Belfast).

Although much occupied with lecturing and administration, Andrews found time to research the nature of gases. One of his early experiments showed that **ozone** was an allotrope (form) of oxygen. Shortly before this discovery ozone had been identified as the gas that produced the strange smell found near an electrical discharge. The word ozone is derived from the Greek *ozon,* meaning to smell or to reek.

The White Linen Hall, Belfast

High Street, Belfast, 1830

Thomas Andrews

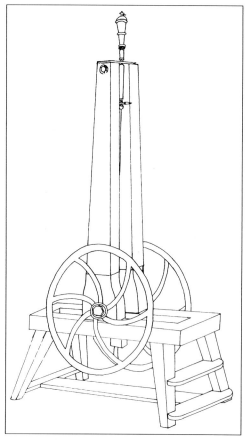

Andrews's large compressor – the steps give an indication of its size (about 1867)

Andrews went on to study what happened to gases when they were put under extremes of pressure at different temperatures. Interestingly, another Irishman, Robert Boyle, the father of modern chemistry, investigated how the volumes of gases are related to their pressures.

By the middle of the 19th century it was thought that certain gases like hydrogen, nitrogen and oxygen could not be changed into liquids, even when they were put under very high pressure (up to 3,000 times atmospheric pressure). These gases were therefore known as **permanent gases**.

Andrews trapped samples of gases in heavy capillary tubes and subjected them to great pressure over a range of temperatures. He found that every gas has a **critical temperature** above which it cannot be turned into a liquid no matter what pressure is exerted on it; below this critical temperature it is quite easy to turn the gas into a liquid.

This discovery by Andrews eventually led to the production of liquid gases. This was a major breakthrough in science and technology, as we can see from a number of today's applications such as rocket fuel, bottled gas, and the cooling fluids in refrigerators.

Andrews was also involved in many social issues. He published work on the function of university education and its role in serving the community, and he was concerned about the higher education of women and of working-class people. He suggested the creation of a department of Celtic at Queen's because he believed that the Irish language should be represented in the university. He wrote an article entitled 'Suggestions for checking the hurtful use of alcoholic beverages by the working classes', which proposed that no public house should have a licence to sell alcohol unless it could provide cooked meals for its customers, and no drink should be sold that contained more than 17% alcohol. He also worked hard to help those who suffered during the Irish potato famine of 1845–9.

During his lifetime Thomas Andrews received many awards and honorary degrees.

DISTINCTIONS and HONORARY DEGREES

1848	Fellow of the Royal Society, London
1849	Member of the Royal Irish Academy
1867	President, education section of the British Association
1870	Honorary fellow of the Royal Society, Edinburgh
1876	Vice-president, Chemical Society of London
	President, the British Association
	Doctor of Laws, Universities of Edinburgh, Glasgow, and Trinity College Dublin
1879	Doctor of Science, the Queen's University in Ireland

In 1880 Andrews was offered a knighthood, but he declined it on the grounds of ill health. He died on 26 November 1885 at Fortwilliam Park, Belfast.

A permanent exhibition of early apparatus, including some of Andrews's original equipment, is on display in the department of chemistry (David Keir Building, Stranmillis Road) of Queen's University Belfast. Adjoining this exhibition area is the Andrews Room, where a large portrait of him hangs.

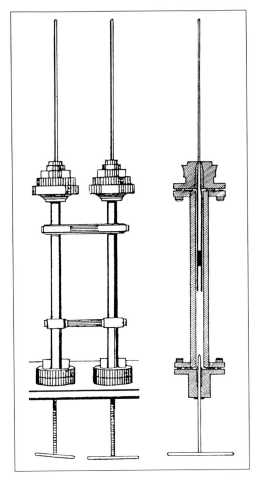

Andrews's small gas compression apparatus, with one of the tubes shown in section

5 Lord Kelvin 1824–1907

Lord Kelvin in his 60s

Places of residence

Belfast 1824–32
Glasgow 1832–41
Cambridge 1841–5
Paris 1845–6
Glasgow 1846–75
Netherhall, Largs, Ayrshire 1875–1907

Family

Father	James Thomson
Mother	Margaret Gardner
Married	Margaret Crum, 1852 (died 1870)
	Frances Anne Blandy, 1874

Lord Kelvin was born William Thomson at 17 College Square East, **Belfast,** on 26 June 1824. His father, James Thomson, was mathematics professor at the Belfast Academical Institution (now RBAI or Inst.), which was situated opposite his birthplace.

The Thomson family had farmed since 1641 in Ballymaglave South, near the Spa, Ballynahinch, County Down, and James was only 12 when the 1798 rebellion broke out. His family supplied provisions to the rebel forces before the battle of Ballynahinch. From a nearby hill they witnessed the defeat of the poorly armed Volunteers and the burning and looting of the town by George III's forces. Many years later young William often spent his boyhood holidays on the farm, playing in the flax fields in full view of the Mountains of Mourne and Slieve Croob.

William was a brilliant child and sometimes attended his father's classes when he was only eight years old. In 1832 his father was appointed professor of mathematics at Glasgow University and at the tender age of just over 10 years, William became a student there. In 1841 he went to Cambridge to continue his studies, graduating in 1845; while there he was a champion rower and one of the founders of the university music society. After studying for a short time under the famous chemist Henri Victor Regnault in Paris, he returned to Glasgow as professor of natural philosophy (the old name for physics) at the early age of 22.

At Glasgow he was one of the first scientists to teach in a laboratory, having converted an old wine cellar in a professor's house. William was different from most of the great scientists at that time, like Michael Faraday and James Clerk Maxwell, in that he believed that his research laboratory would help him to apply his knowledge of physics to the needs of industry, which was growing rapidly in the 19th century.

Thomson's first investigations were concerned with mechanical work and energy loss, no doubt encouraged by his older brother James (professor of civil engineering at Glasgow since 1873), who had designed more efficient engines for steamships. Over the next 10 years William published some of his best-known scientific achievements, many based on the concept of heat and work.

Thomson supported James Joule's theory of the equivalence of heat and mechanical energy, and together they discovered the **Joule–Thomson effect,** which concerned the manner in which the temperatures of gases drop when they expand in a vacuum. Later this effect was important to Sir James Dewar, who obtained ultra-low temperatures to liquefy some of the permanent gases. (Incidentally, Dewar's research was also influenced by Thomas Andrews.) Thomson's investigations formed the basis of modern low-temperature engineering, such as the making of liquid oxygen and liquid nitrogen. He also demonstrated the application of the reversible heat engine to refrigeration.

In 1846 Thomson made the first scientific calculation of the age of the earth, challenging the biblical fundamentalists who claimed it began 6,000 years ago, and the biologist Charles Darwin who claimed it was almost infinitely old. Thomson's calculation of about 100 million years was based on the cooling of the earth, assuming that at one time it had the same temperature as the sun. Before he died the discovery of radioactive elements in the earth's crust led to our modern estimate of over 4,000 million years.

AWARDS and HONOURS	
1846–1852	Fellow of Peterhouse College, Cambridge
1851	Fellow of the Royal Society, London
1868	Fellow of the Royal Astronomical Society
1871	President, the British Association
1872–1907	Fellow of Peterhouse College, Cambridge
1873	President, the Royal Society, Edinburgh
1878	President, the Royal Society, Edinburgh
1881	Commander, Légion d'honneur
1886	President, the British Association
1888–1889	President, the Mathematical Society of London
1889	Grand Officer, Légion d'honneur
1890	President, the Royal Society, Edinburgh
1890–1895	President, the Royal Society, London
1892	Created Lord Kelvin of Largs Vice-president and Manager, the Royal Institute
1895	President, the Royal Society, Edinburgh
1902	Privy councillor of Great Britain Order of merit
1904	Chancellor of Glasgow University
1907	President, the Royal Society, Edinburgh

Lord Kelvin

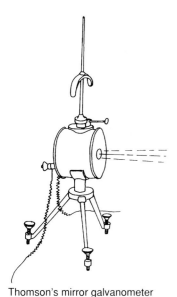

Thomson's mirror galvanometer

The Thomson compass

Thomson played a major part in the plans for the laying of the transatlantic telegraph cable linking Ireland with Canada. He was a fervent imperialist and saw this as a physical union between parts of the British Empire. The first cable had failed in 1857, so Thomson approached the problem in a thoroughly scientific way. In his laboratory he studied the effects of the resistance and capacitance of an insulated copper cable on the slowing down of the electric signal, and calculated the best dimensions for the thickness of the cable. He designed precise testing instruments and an ingenious galvanometer which automatically recorded the signals at the other end.

Thomson was the first of a new generation of scientific engineers who recognised the harmony between theory and practice, economy and design. His insistence on an exact system of electrical units led to the founding of the National Physical Laboratory. With the success of the transatlantic cable he was awarded a knighthood in 1866.

William Thomson was a shrewd financial genius; he accumulated a massive fortune through his patents and business interests. In 1870 he purchased a large yacht and became interested in the problems of navigation. Ships' compasses used before 1880 consisted of a pivoted magnet under a heavy card. They were very sluggish and inclined to stick and were useless in stormy weather or on a battleship during gunfire. With the increase in the number of iron ships, compasses were proving unsatisfactory because they were affected by the metal. Thomson designed a new improved compass which consisted of eight narrow steel needles suspended from a light aluminium ring under a thin circular card. During the bombardment of Alexandria on 11 July 1882 the captains of two British warships reported that the new compass was far superior to any previous compasses. It was then adopted by all British navy vessels.

William's brother James had invented a remarkable calculating machine and Thomson adapted it to predict the height of the tide at any place and date. He also introduced a new type of depth-sounding apparatus by which soundings could be taken while a ship was still moving.

As a young man of 24, he had investigated Charles's discovery that gases lose $1/273$ of their 0°C volume for every 1°C drop in temperature. He proposed that it was not the volume but the energy of motion of the molecules of the gas which reached zero at −273°C. He called this temperature **absolute zero**, and the new scale of temperature the **absolute scale.** After he became Lord Kelvin of Largs in 1892, it was known as the **Kelvin scale,** the standard of temperature measurement under the modern Système International d'Unités (SI units).

Despite Kelvin's magnificent achievements and his astonishing mind, he failed to make the ultimate advances in some of his researches. It is thought that he did not pay enough attention to other people's work. His individualism may be due to the fact that he did not go to school but was taught at home and so missed out on the opportunity to work and co-operate with others. With a little more discipline he might have become what many thought him to be – a second Isaac Newton.

He died on 17 December 1907 and was buried beside Newton in Westminster Abbey on 23 December.

A statue unveiled in his honour at the Botanic Gardens, Belfast, in 1913 has this inscription: *'He elucidated the laws of nature for the service of man.'*

Commemorative statue of Lord Kelvin in the Botanic Gardens, Belfast

6 Mary Ward 1827–1869

Mary Ward

Places of residence

Ballylin, Ferbane, King's County 1827–57
Trimbleston, Booterstown, County Dublin
  1857–61
Bellair, Moate, King's County 1861–4
Kingstown, County Dublin 1864–9

Family

Father   The Reverend Henry King
Mother   Harriette Lloyd
Married   Henry William Crosbie Ward, 1854
Children Three sons and five daughters

Mary Ward was born Mary King on 27 April 1827 at Ballylin on the outskirts of Ferbane in King's County (now County Offaly); she was the youngest of four children, having a brother and two sisters.

She belonged to an aristocratic family and was a first cousin of the famous astronomer William Parsons (the 3rd Earl of Rosse). Instead of going to school she received her early education at home from a governess. She lived about 15 miles from Birr Castle and often visited there, where she met many of the distinguished scientists of the day.

From a young age the girls in the family showed a keen interest in natural history and astronomy and became capable entomologists, ornithologists and botanists. Mary particularly liked using a magnifying glass to look at small natural objects, and then to draw them. Her parents encouraged this activity and when she was 18 her father bought her a microscope, a beautiful instrument made by Ross of London. It had been recommended by the astronomer Sir James South, a frequent visitor to Birr Castle, and at that time it was probably the finest microscope in Ireland.

Mary described the microscope thus: *'When upright [it] is almost one foot ten inches high, but it has a joint that enables it to lean back, so that I can look through it and draw what I see quite conveniently . . . There are three eye glasses and five object glasses of different magnifying power . . . There is a little looking glass to reflect the light of a window or a candle if the object is partially transparent, for the most important thing in managing a microscope is to place the objects in the clearest light or else we cannot find out the truth about them.'*

Naturalist & Artist

Mary searched the scientific literature for information on microscopy and gradually learned how to prepare objects for examination under the microscope.

In 1854 Mary married the Honourable Henry William Crosbie Ward, of **Castle Ward**, near **Strangford** in County Down. The family usually stayed at Castle Ward during the holidays. Mary was an excellent artist, and even though she was busy looking after her home, husband and eight children (only six reached adulthood), she observed, drew and painted birds, fish and insects.

She illustrated several books and scientific articles by Sir David Brewster, the Scottish physicist who invented the kaleidoscope. She was, however, especially fascinated by what she saw under her microscope, and she often worked late at night when the children were in bed.

Being a woman, she could not at that time become a member of any learned societies or institutions or obtain any degrees or diplomas. (Edinburgh University was the first to admit women in 1869.) It was not until the latter part of the 19th century that women became recognised for scientific or literary work.

As early as 1856 Mary decided to make her scientific investigations available to others. She had an article – 'A windfall for the microscope' – published privately, and by the time she was 30 she decided to publish a book of her drawings. In 1857 it was very difficult to find a publisher who would accept work from women, so her first book – *Sketches with the Microscope* – was also published privately. However, it was published the following year by Groomsbridge of London as *The World of Wonders as Revealed by the Microscope* (the author was described as

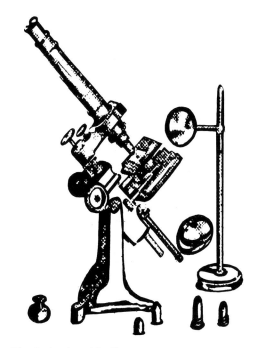

Mary's drawing of the Ross microscope and accessories

Mary Ward

The Insect Maypole by Mary Ward (postcard issued by the National Trust in Northern Ireland)

'The Hon. Mrs W'). The book was very successful, being reprinted at least eight times in various forms between 1858 and 1888.

At that time good but affordable microscopes and telescopes were becoming widely available so that microscopy and astronomy became popular hobbies. In 1864 Mary's book was enlarged, revised, and published as *Microscope Teachings: Descriptions of Various Objects of Especial Interest and Beauty Adapted for Microscopic Observation.* It described more advanced microscope techniques in a clear and concise way, including details of how microscope slides were prepared for examination.

Mary Ward was one of the best-known 19th-century writers on the use of the microscope. Her books were a breath of fresh air, being simply written and beautifully illustrated; they appealed to all ages, were quite cheap, and sold well. Two of her books were chosen to go on display in the book section of the International Exhibition at the famous Crystal Palace in 1862.

In 1845 the 3rd Earl of Rosse built the world's largest telescope in the grounds of Birr Castle. Mary observed and described the construction of this massive instrument. The main tube of the telescope held a metal mirror that was six feet in diameter and weighed four tons. Recently the tube has been restored at Birr Castle but the mirror had already been removed to the Science Museum in London, where it still remains. Using this telescope, Mary's cousin discovered that nebulae were spiral. Later she published articles and books on astronomy, one being *Telescope Teachings* in 1859.

Mary corresponded with Sir William Rowan Hamilton, the

Mary Ward

Astronomer-Royal of Ireland, who held her in high esteem; he sent her his personal copies of *Monthly Notices of the Royal Astronomical Society*. In 1862 she visited Greenwich Observatory – a most unusual occurrence at that time for a woman. It gives some idea of the regard in which she was held.

On 31 August 1869 Mary was travelling on a steam carriage (developed by Lord Rosse) with her husband and two of Lord Rosse's sons when it hit a bump; Mary was thrown out, one of the wheels ran over her and she died instantly. Her early death was tragic – she would surely have gone on to become a leading authority on microscopy, which would have contributed greatly to the increasingly significant role of women in science. In a few years' time she would have become the 5th Viscountess Bangor and would have had more free time to devote to, and develop, her scientific work.

After Mary's death her family came to live at Castle Ward and the children were brought up there. It is now administered by the National Trust in Northern Ireland and a room has been set up there as a permanent exhibition of Mary Ward's work. Her microscope and accessories, slides, some manuscripts and books are on display.

Castle Ward House, Strangford, County Down

Epitaph by an anonymous writer:
'She was distinguished alike by her talents and energy, her scientific acquirements, her genial and affectionate disposition and her many virtues.'

John Boyd Dunlop in his late 40s

Places of residence

Dreghorn, Ayrshire 1840–67
Gloucester Street, Belfast 1867–92
Blackrock, County Dublin 1892–1921

Family

Father Not known
Mother Not known
Married Miss McCormack, 1876
Children One son and one daughter

John Boyd Dunlop was born on 5 February 1840 in the village of Dreghorn (Ayrshire, Scotland) of tenant farmer stock. He attended the local parish school and was such a good student that he often helped out as a pupil teacher. He progressed to the nearby Irvine Academy and qualified as a veterinary surgeon when he was only 19.

He moved to **Belfast** in his late 20s to set up a veterinary practice at 50 Gloucester Street, off May Street. This was a thriving district in those days, being near the busy heart of the city and the large Markets area, where farm animals were bought and sold. Horse-drawn jaunting cars, carriages, trams and carts filled the city streets.

Dr John Fagan, founder of the Belfast Children's Hospital (he was knighted in 1910), often called at the veterinary establishment, for Dr Fagan treated Dunlop's son Johnny, and Dunlop looked after Dr Fagan's animals. Dunlop was worried about his son's health, and Dr Fagan suggested that cycling would be good exercise for him. At that time the streets of Belfast were paved with granite blocks and cobblestones, which made them very bumpy. Cycling on solid-tyred wheels was a boneshaking experience, which Johnny complained about, although he often raced his schoolmates on his tricycle.

Johnny asked his father if he could make his tricycle go more smoothly. The matter was discussed at length; Dunlop came up with the idea of replacing the solid tyre with a hosepipe filled with water, but Fagan suggested filling the tube with air instead, probably because he had some experience of working with air cushions and mattresses at the hospital.

Dunlop used the idea of an inflated hollow tube providing

a cushion of air between the wheel and the ground, and designed a simple experiment to test it. He made a tube from thin rubber sheet and fixed this to a wooden wheel with strips of linen from one of his wife's old dresses. Then, using a teat from a baby's bottle as a valve, he blew the tube up with a football pump. He rolled the wheel down his back yard and found that instead of toppling over like the solid-tyred wheel of his son's tricycle, it travelled the length of the yard and bounced off the wall.

Dunlop developed this concept by fitting inflated tubes covered in canvas jackets to two three-foot-diameter wooden hoops. These he wrapped in an outer jacket of rubber sheeting strengthened with two extra strips of rubber on the threads. Everything was bonded together with rubber solution, and the tyres stuck to the rim. The wooden hoops were then fixed to the two large rear wheels of Johnny's tricycle with copper wire. The job was finished on 28 February 1888, and on that evening young Johnny had a secret trial run. He soon discovered that his new tyres were much better – not only was the ride smoother but he could also go much faster so that he won most of the races he had with his schoolmates.

After further improvements Dunlop applied for a patent for his invention – patent number 10607 of 1888: '*An Improvement in Tyres of Wheels for Bicycles, Tricycles or other Road Cars . . . A hollow tyre or tube made of india-rubber and cloth, or other suitable material, said tube or tyre to contain air under pressure or otherwise and to be attached to the wheel or wheels in such a method as may be found most suitable.*' Dunlop was the first person to apply the word **pneumatic** to tyres. In fact, the pneumatic tyre had been invented in 1845 by another Scot, Robert W.

A reconstruction of Johnny's tricycle, with the new pneumatic tyres fitted to the large back wheels

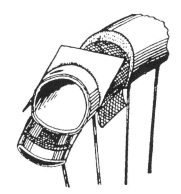

The 'mummy' tyre; patent number 4116 of 1889

John Boyd Dunlop

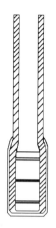

Dunlop's valve; patent number 4115 of 1889

Dunlop was very striking in appearance – he had the air and looks of an Old Testament patriarch. His face, with flowing white beard, was used for many years as the trademark of the Dunlop Rubber Company.

Thompson, so although Dunlop was not the originator of the idea, he was responsible for devising practical applications for its use by bringing together those elements that were required for success – the use of vulcanised rubber for the tyres, a method of attaching them to the wheel rims, and a valve for inflating them (basically the same as the modern tyre).

In the late 19th century there was heated debate over whether the penny-farthing cycle was better than the new safety cycle, which had two smaller but equal-sized wheels. The Dunlop tyre could be fitted more easily to the safety cycle, but because the new tyres were wider than the solid ones, they would not run between the forks of existing machines. Special frames, therefore, had to be built, and Dunlop asked W. Edlin and Company of Belfast to make cycles using tyres to his patent. Even though the valve mechanism, the tyre materials and the frame were improved, a major problem still remained – how to make the new pneumatic tyre appealing to cyclists.

Although Dunlop's main interest in the development of pneumatic tyres was comfort, the bonus of extra speed boosted publicity for the invention. In those days cycle racing was very popular. On 18 May 1889 a race was held at the Queen's College (now Queen's University) playing fields at Cherryvale and one of the entrants, Willie Hume, captain of the Belfast Cruiser Cycle Club, agreed to use a bicycle fitted with Dunlop's tyres. When the bicycle appeared on the track the crowd roared with laughter because its 'sausage' tyres looked so clumsy compared to the neat-looking solid rubber ones. However, Hume won the race to the astonishment not only of the spectators but also of some of his more fancied competitors.

The demand for pneumatic safety cycles grew so quickly that Dunlop ended his association with Edlin, went to Dublin and teamed up with Bowden and Gillies to start a new, but larger, company.

The foundation of the **Dunlop Rubber Company** can be traced back to Hume's victory at Cherryvale, for among the spectators that day was Harvey du Cros, a Dublin paper merchant whose sons were among the well-known cyclists who had been defeated. He saw the commercial possibilities of these new tyres and in 1896 he bought Dunlop's patents and business for £3 million and his son, Arthur Philip du Cros, took over as managing director. The company expanded and moved to Dale Street in Coventry, then the main manufacturing centre for cycles. There it played a key role in the development of the pneumatic tyre industry as the motorcar became popular.

Dunlop was always concerned about his health and he often suffered from colds. He died unexpectedly, following a slight chill, on 24 October 1921. His name lives on in the Dunlop Company, which still makes tyres and sports equipment.

Two early Edlin pneumatic safety cycles are on display in the Ulster Museum, Stranmillis Road, Belfast. Some early cycles and a penny-farthing with Dunlop tyres can be seen at the Ulster Folk and Transport Museum, Cultra.

A £10 note featuring John Boyd Dunlop was issued by the Northern Bank in August 1990.

The grand old gentleman on his bike at the annual meet of the Irish Cyclists' Old Timers Fellowship in Dublin, 1918

The present trademark of the Dunlop Company

8 Robert Lloyd Praeger   1865–1953

Robert Lloyd Praeger

Places of residence
Holywood, County Down 1865–93
31 Upper Baggot Street, Dublin 1893–1902
Lisnane, Zion Road, Rathgar, Dublin
 1902–22
19 Fitzwilliam Square, Dublin 1922–52
Rock Cottage, Craigavad, County Down
 1952–3

Family
Father   Willem E. Praeger
Mother   Maria Patterson
Married   Hedwig Magnusson, 1901

Robert Lloyd Praeger was born at Woodburn in **Holywood**, County Down, on 25 August 1865. He showed an interest in nature from a very early age; when he was old enough to toddle, his father had to put a fence around the garden at the front of the house because he picked the flowers. Before he was even five he could recognise belemnites, bluebells and flint-flakes.

He first attended a small private school before going to the Royal Belfast Academical Institution. By this time he knew a great deal about local plants – where they grew, when they blossomed, what their roots and seeds were like, as well as the structure of their flowers. At Inst. he eagerly joined a botany class that met once a fortnight. However, he found that it *consisted in drawing a series of adnate parallelograms and entering in the blank spaces such terms as "monochlamydeous" and "gamosepalous". I fled in terror, and later, at college, I did not venture again to approach my favourite subject as seen through the eyes of a teacher of Victoria's glorious days.'*

When he was 11 his father encouraged him to join the **Belfast Naturalists' Field Club**, which had been founded by his grandfather, Robert Patterson, in 1863. It was made up of enthusiastic amateurs who had a remarkably good knowledge of local biology and geology, and young Praeger soon came under their stimulating influence. He was befriended by S.A. Stewart, who *'was tireless in naming specimens and in imparting all that lore relating to botanical and geological field-work that is not to be found in any book but which passes from mouth to mouth among those who keep the torch of knowledge burning. No young naturalist ever had a better, or more patient teacher, or a more delightful friend.'* It was his field club training that gave

Botanist & Naturalist

Praeger such a deep interest in all natural phenomena in Ireland.

In the autumn of 1882 he went to Queen's College, and attended lectures in arts and engineering. He found Queen's to be a rather forbidding place where practical work in laboratories was confined to chemistry and anatomy courses. He was awarded a Bachelor of Arts degree in 1885, and one year later he graduated in engineering. He studied geology as part of the engineering course, but never had the chance to handle a rock specimen or a fossil. *'Anyway,'* he said, *'I always preferred the field as my laboratory.'*

His first job was as a civil engineer with the Belfast Water Commissioners, when the Alexandra Dock was being built. At this time he studied the fossil shells which were being unearthed during excavation and in 1886 he wrote his first paper – 'Notes on the sections recently exposed at Alexandra Docks'. This was the start of a life devoted to nature and to writing about it.

Since his real love was plants, he gave up his engineering job after five years to work with Canon Grainger of Broughshane, County Antrim, on his plant collection. He went to Dublin in 1893 to work as an assistant librarian in the National Library of Ireland, where he eventually became chief librarian in 1920. In 1923 he retired on full pension; this allowed him more time to write and to follow several lines of research.

In 1894 he put forward a scheme to divide Ireland into 40 **divisions** and to work out the range of every flowering plant in them. In 1905 he organised a survey of Lambay Island to study the *'natural production – animal, vegetable and mineral'* of the island. The findings were published in

Members of the Belfast Naturalists' Field Club, *c.* 1890; Praeger is standing in the centre, wearing a bowler hat

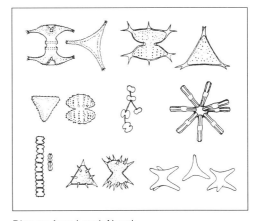

Diatoms from Lough Neagh

Robert Lloyd Praeger

Lambay and Clare Islands

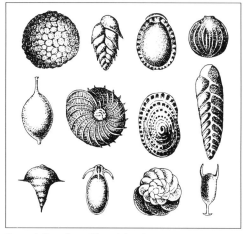

Foraminifera from Clare Island

the *Irish Naturalist*: he listed 5 new animal species, 12 others new to the British fauna, and 90 animals and plants never before recorded in Ireland.

From 1909 to 1922 he organised a survey of Clare Island, where he found 1,253 animal species previously unrecorded in Ireland, of which 343 were new to the British Isles and 109 new to science; of the 3,219 plants collected, 585 were new to Ireland, 55 new to the British Isles and 11 new to science.

Praeger was probably the most important field botanist who has ever worked in Ireland. He was also widely recognised for his contributions to archaeology, Quaternary geology, phytogeography, zoology, history and librarianship, and he received many honours and distinctions.

He hiked all over Ireland, studying and collecting plants, and he was a prolific writer. He produced a total of 24 books and numerous articles and papers. In 1895 *The Botanist in Ireland* was published. This became a standard work for over 50 years on Irish flowering plants, ferns and stoneworts. He was in many respects like an early David Bellamy.

One of his best-loved books, *The Way That I Went*, which first appeared in 1937, has been reprinted many times and is still available in paperback; it is written for the layperson and is well worth reading. In the Preface, Praeger says of the book: *'It is, indeed, a kind of thank-offering, however crude, for seven decades of robust physical health in which to walk and climb and swim and sail throughout or around the island in which I was born, to the benefit alike of body and soul.'*

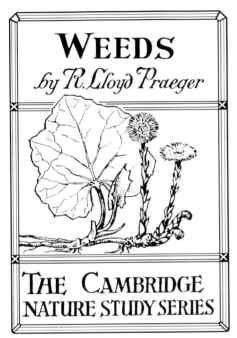

A particularly interesting book is *Weeds: Simple Lessons for Children*, published in 1913 as part of the Cambridge Nature Study series; it was illustrated by his sister Rosamond, an artist and sculptor, and R.J. Welch, the well-known photographer.

Praeger has been described as *'a man of vast experience, boundless energy and encyclopaedic knowledge, of great integrity, whose kindly nature was concealed by a gruff manner'*. He was active well into his 80s and was proud of his vitality in old age.

He depicted Ireland as *'a very lovely country'*, but he regretted that *'the people who are in it have not the common-sense to live in peace with one another and with their neighbours'*.

Praeger died at Rock Cottage, his sister's home, in Craigavad, County Down, on 5 May 1953.

DISTINCTIONS and HONORARY DEGREES	
1914	President, the Belfast Naturalists' Field Club
1921	Veitch Gold Medal, the Royal Horticultural Society of Ireland
1923	President, the British Ecological Society
1927	Gold Medal, the Belfast Naturalists' Field Club
1931– 1934	President, the Royal Irish Academy
1932	Veitch Gold Medal, the Royal Horticultural Society of Ireland
1934	President, the Geographical Society of Ireland
1940	Gold Medal, the Royal Horticultural Society of Ireland
1941	President, the Royal Zoological Society of Ireland
1947	Associate member, the Linnaean Society
1948	First President, An Taisce (the National Trust for Ireland)
1949– 1950	President, the Royal Horticultural Society of Ireland
1950	Vice-president, the Royal Dublin Society
1951	Honorary life member, the Botanical Society of the British Isles
	Honorary doctorates from a number of universities

Harry Ferguson in his early 50s

Places of residence

Growell, Hillsborough, County Down
  1884–1902
Belfast, England, USA and Canada 1902–48
Abbotswood, Stow-on-the-Wold 1948–60

Family

Father	James Ferguson
Mother	Mary Bell
Married	Maureen Watson, 1913
Children	One daughter

34

Harry George Ferguson was born on 4 November 1884 at Lake House in the townland of Growell near **Hillsborough** in County Down. He was the fourth son in a family of eleven children. His father, a farmer, was a member of the Plymouth Brethren. The Fergusons could trace their family in Ireland back to the plantations from Scotland in the early 17th century.

Harry, as he was always known, left the local school at the age of 14 to work on his father's farm. Curiously, the Industrial Revolution had largely bypassed agriculture, so that horses were still the only source of power in ploughing. Life was a relentless grind; the produce, and thus the profits, were small.

When he was 17 Harry decided that farming was not for him, and he left home to work for his older brother Joe, who had started up a small car- and cycle-repair business in Little Donegall Street, Belfast.

It soon became clear that Harry had a talent for understanding the mysteries of the new petrol engines, so he attended evening classes in engineering at the Belfast Technical College (in 1991 it became part of the new Belfast Institute of Further and Higher Education).

The small firm gained a reputation for quality and reliability, and Harry took part in sporting events for publicity purposes. He achieved many successes in motorbike and motorcar races.

Harry had heard stories about the first aeroplane flights of the Wright brothers and Blériot. In 1909 he attended the Blackpool Air Show and afterwards decided to build and fly his own aeroplane. The result was a remarkable achievement since he had no reference books or plans to work from. He first tested his new aeroplane on Lord Downshire's estate in Hillsborough, and after several failures and modifications, he succeeded in flying 130 yards at a height of 15 feet on 31 December 1909. He thus became the first Briton to design and build a monoplane.

In July 1910 he made a number of short flights of about one mile each on Magilligan strand in County Londonderry. In August 1910, after many unsuccessful attempts to overcome the strong air currents around the Mountains of Mourne, he won a prize of £100 for flying more than three miles over Newcastle, County Down, at a height of 100 feet. He became known as the 'mad mechanic' because he was so determined and fearless. He eventually gave up flying at the request of his wife.

In 1911 Harry set up his own garage business – the May Street Motor Company. The firm prospered and took on agencies for Vauxhall and Ford cars. In 1914 he started to sell Overtime tractors imported from America. These early tractors were heavy, clumsy and expensive. If the implement being towed caught in an obstruction in the soil, the tractor was inclined to overturn and crush the unfortunate driver.

The effects of the submarine blockade during the First World War (1914–18) created a national crisis, and there was a need to increase home food production to prevent starvation. Farmers were asked to till up to 20% more land, although they did not have the extra manpower or the horses to do so. In March 1917 the Government managed to import 6,000 Ford tractors from America, and the Irish Board of Agriculture asked Ferguson to investigate ways of improving the efficiency and quality of tractor ploughing.

Ferguson and his monoplane at Magilligan strand in 1910

Business card

Harry Ferguson

The 'Wee Fergie' (TE-20)

Harry realised that, if farming was to progress, not only were better-designed tractors and ploughs needed but also some new method of connecting the two together had to be found. He designed and built a new-style plough for the Ford tractor in his May Street garage. Apart from its simplicity and lightness, this machine was unique in one very important way – the tractor and the plough formed a single unit. It was the birth of the unit system, or the **Ferguson System**, which is now used on tractors all over the world. Another significant advance was that the depth of ploughing could be controlled from the driver's seat.

Harry further improved his plough by adding a hydraulic system, and in 1933 he designed his own tractor, which was very light and powerful. The first production models of the Ferguson tractor were made by David Brown of Huddersfield in 1936, and sold for £224 each.

In October 1938 the Ferguson System was demonstrated to the famous Henry Ford at Dearborn, USA. Ford was impressed and agreed to manufacture the Ferguson model if Harry took charge of design work and sales. The new tractor was ready in 1939 and sold well. By 1947, 300,000 Ford Fergusons had been built.

In 1946, with British government backing, a new model, the TE-20 was built by the Standard Motor Company in England, and by 1956 over 500,000 of these 'Wee Fergies' had been sold.

Harry's company merged with a large firm in Toronto, Canada – Massey-Harris – to form Massey-Ferguson. In 1954, at the age of 70, he resigned as chairman.

Still full of zest, he returned to his great interest in motorcars. Realising that with four-wheel drive he could develop a safer, more powerful car, he built a racing car that was driven successfully by the legendary racing driver, Stirling Moss. Unfortunately, Harry could not find a manufacturer to produce a model using four-wheel drive for wide public use. The concept was, however, used in a luxury sports coupé – the Jensen Interceptor FF. He also invented a device for preventing the locking of wheels in a skid. Both these innovations have recently become popular on production cars such as the Ford Sierra – once again, Harry was well ahead of his time.

In many ways he was a fascinating man: obsessed with efficiency, energetic, always determined to overcome any obstacles put in his way. He was an individual whose vitality was fuelled by a magnificent dream – to solve the massive problem of worldwide food shortage.

Harry Ferguson refused a knighthood for his services to the Allies during the Second World War. He died suddenly on 25 October 1960 at his estate home in the Cotswolds.

A full-scale replica of Ferguson's aeroplane, an early Ferguson-Brown tractor and Sherman-Ferguson plough are on display in the Ulster Folk and Transport Museum at Cultra. Commemorative plaques are displayed at Growell and the former premises of Harry Ferguson Limited in Donegall Square East, Belfast.

The Northern Bank issued a £20 note featuring Harry Ferguson in August 1990.

Ford Sierra

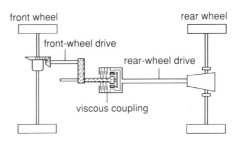

Four-wheel drive of the Ford Sierra, based on Ferguson's system

In Welsh, the word for 'tractor' is *fergie* – a man could ask little better as a tribute.

10 Sir James Martin   1893–1981

Sir James Martin

James Martin was born on 11 September 1893 at **Crossgar** in County Down. He was the only son of Thomas, a farmer, who died when James was two years of age. He inherited an inventing streak from his father, who had designed farming implements and an advanced bicycle. When James was young he spent much of his time tinkering with different mechanical devices. As a teenager he devised, built and sold a wide variety of machines, and by hard work and study became a capable engineer before he was 20. He refused a place at Queen's University to study engineering, preferring to be outside inventing and making things. In his early 20s he designed a three-wheeled enclosed car as a cheap runabout, and small oil engines for various uses.

In 1924 James set off for London with only £10 in his pocket and there he stayed with his sister. He was determined to set up his own business and he soon found a small shed in Acton at a low rent. He applied his remarkable gifts in design and engineering to developing and marketing a range of machines – from small oil engines to specialised vehicles of all kinds. He was inventor, draughtsman, experimental engineer, tool-maker, fitter, assemblyman, salesman and delivery driver. He liked fast cars and even raced at the famous racetrack, Brooklands; in 1928 he entered the International Tourist Trophy race round the Ards circuit but, unfortunately, he crashed on the fourth lap.

The company expanded and in 1929 moved to Denham in Middlesex. Now called the Martin Aircraft Works, its aim was to build simpler and better aeroplanes. Resources were meagre – two employees, a few machine tools and some engineering equipment – but these problems were overcome by James's technical skill, forceful personality and energy.

Places of residence

Killinchy Woods, Crossgar, County Down
  1893–1924
London 1924–9
Southlands Manor, Denham, Middlesex
  1929–81

Family

Father   Thomas Martin
Mother   Sarah Coulter
Married   Muriel Haines, 1942
Children Twin sons and two daughters

38

Inventor

The company's first plane, the MB1, was a small, strong but light, single-engined two-seater monoplane for civilian use, made with thin steel tubing covered in fabric. Successful flight trials were completed but no orders were placed. In 1934 Captain Val Baker, James's flying instructor at the London Aeroplane Club and a good friend, joined the company as chief test pilot. The Martin-Baker Company, as it was now called, switched to designing fighters for the Royal Air Force – the MB2, first flown in 1938, and the MB3, to replace the famous Hurricane and Spitfire fighters. The MB3 was first flown by Captain Baker on 31 August 1942, but during a flight on 12 September the engine seized and Baker was killed trying to land in a small field. This tragedy was probably the main reason why Martin dedicated himself to finding ways of saving pilots' lives. Despite this setback he developed the MB4 and the MB5, both excellent aircraft that had the approval of pilots and ground crews. However, the RAF did not place any orders.

Meanwhile the company was converting many of Martin's ideas into products – armaments like blast tubes and gun mountings, flat-feed systems for cannon and a barrage-balloon cable cutter. The cable of the barrage balloon moved along the edge of the plane's wing until it slid into a groove, where it was sliced through by a fired chisel; 250,000 cable cutters were made during the Second World War and used with great success. Indeed, aircraft even severed cables on night raids, with the aircrews unaware of the fact until they returned to base.

During the Battle of Britain many pilots were unable to escape from their cockpits because the canopies would not always slide back when damaged. Martin devised a way of blowing the canopy off the aircraft, thus giving the pilot a clear escape.

The MB5 fighter aircraft

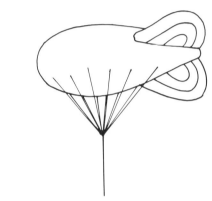

Barrage balloon, used by both Britain and Germany during the Second World War to prevent attacks by low-flying enemy aircraft

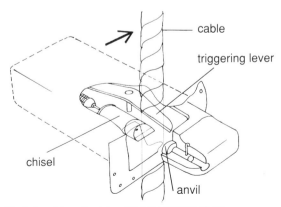

cable

triggering lever

chisel

anvil

Martin's cable cutter (simplified diagram to show triggering lever, chisel and anvil)

Sir James Martin

Bailing out

1. The pilot pulls the ejection handle, setting off a series of explosive charges which blasts the canopy and the pilot out of the jet.

2. The thrust of the blast drives the pilot 90 to 120 metres skyward and fires a drogue parachute.

3. The drogue parachute slows down the pilot, stabilises the seat and deploys the main parachute.

4. The main parachute opens and automatically releases the ejection seat from the pilot.

5. A life raft and survival kit are deployed. The kit includes food, a knife, water, a medical kit, a two-way radio and other supplies.

By 1943, however, fighter aircraft were flying much faster and the jet engine was coming on the scene. Escaping 'over the side' was becoming impossible because of the surrounding air pressures; if the pilot did manage to get out he was likely to be struck by some part of the aircraft.

In 1944 Martin was invited by the Ministry of Aircraft Production to develop some means of improving the survival rate of pilots. His first theory was demonstrated to Sir Stafford Cripps using a model – a powerful spring and a swinging arm to lift the pilot out of the aircraft. Official backing was secured, and in 1945 the concept was further developed – a dummy pilot *and* his seat were forceably ejected using explosive charges.

The whole idea was hazardous since no one knew how the human body would withstand the huge forces involved. These forces were reduced by using a minor explosion to start the seat moving, followed by a greater explosion to accelerate the seat clear of the aircraft. He experimented with sandbags and then fired human volunteers up test rigs. He also worked out the safest sitting position for pilots when they were being shot out. A few seconds after leaving the aircraft the seat and the pilot automatically separated and the pilot's parachute opened.

The first live shot, from a plane, using the ejector seat was undertaken by Bernard Lynch (one of the company's experimental fitters) and it took place on 24 July 1946 from a Gloster Meteor jet. The system worked so well that by June 1947 MB ejector seats were being fitted in all new British military jet aircraft.

The first ground-level ejection took place on 3 September 1955. The US Navy brought Martin to America in August 1957 to demonstrate the efficiency of his system and he was so convincing that MB seats were fitted to all US carrier-borne aircraft. Shortly afterwards they were installed in all NATO aircraft.

Martin continued to develop the ejector seat for use at higher speeds, at greater altitudes, during vertical take-off, in multiple crew escape and in underwater ejection. The Martin-Baker Company was also involved in the production of automatic life raft and life-vest inflation units for more than 400 types of aircraft. In February 1983 the 5,000th life was saved using the MB ejector seat, which is now in use with the airforces and navies of over 50 countries. The total number of lives saved increases at an average rate of more than three per week.

Sir James died at his Middlesex home on 5 January 1981; he was still managing director and chief designer of the company he founded. His twin sons, James and John, are now on the board of directors, and the company has remained in private ownership. In the 1980s the firm formed Aerospace Seating, a company producing crash-resistant airline passenger seats. The call for this type of seat emerged from the horrific Kegworth air disaster of 1989. Martin-Baker still retains close links with Northern Ireland through the Langford Lodge Engineering Company near Crumlin in County Antrim, where one of MB's rocket-propelled sledges is used for high-speed tests. A Mark 3 ejector seat is on display at the Ulster Folk and Transport Museum at Cultra.

James Martin was a very hard-working man: up to his death he could be found at his desk six days a week; he did not take holidays, and was even known to work on Christmas Day. The company he founded dominates the world market and should continue to do so for a long time to come.

AWARDS and HONOURS

1950 Officer of the Order of the British Empire
1951 Wakefield Gold Medal of the Royal Aeronautical Society
1957 Commander of the Order of the British Empire
1958 Laura Taber Barbour Air Safety Award
1959 Cumberbatch Air Safety Trophy
1964 Royal Aero Club Gold Medal
1965 Knight Bachelor
1970 Doctor of Science, Queen's University Belfast
1975 Doctor of Science, College of Aeronautics, Cranfield

A fitting memorial plaque by the Engineering Council to commemorate Sir James Martin was unveiled by his sons on 25 May 1988 in the Square in Crossgar.

In August 1990 the Northern Bank issued a £100 note featuring Sir James Martin.

Ernest Walton

Places of residence

Dungarvan, County Waterford 1903–12
Methodist Manse, Cookstown, County Tyrone
  1912–15
Methodist College, Belfast 1915–22
Dublin 1922–7
Cambridge 1927–34
26 St Kevin's Park, Dublin 1934–

Family

Father	The Reverend John Arthur Walton
Mother	Ann Elizabeth Sinton
Married	Winifred Isabel Wilson, 1934
Children	Two sons and two daughters

Ernest Thomas Sinton Walton was born in Dungarvan, County Waterford, on 6 October 1903. His father, a Methodist minister, had to move from place to place every few years. His mother was from Tandragee in County Armagh.

When Ernest was nine the family moved to the Methodist manse in **Cookstown**, County Tyrone. He attended the local school, Cookstown Academy, until he was 12 and then he was sent to Methodist College Belfast (Methody) as a boarder. During the First World War (1914–18) the German submarine menace prevented many parents from sending their sons and daughters to boarding schools in Britain so that the school was filled to overflowing.

The headmaster of Methody, Mr Henderson, recognised the importance of science and engineering in an industrialised society like Northern Ireland, and he built workshops and laboratories to provide a continuous supply of *'virile, earnest young men who could be trained for posts of responsibility'*.

At Methody young Walton developed an interest in science and mathematics. He also gained skills in woodwork and metalwork by reading and working with a variety of tools in his spare time.

Ernest studied hard and did well in his exams. When he was 19 he went to Trinity College Dublin – an elegant university in a trouble-torn city, since Ireland was engaged in a civil war.

He obtained his first degree in mathematics in 1926. The following year he was awarded the highly prized 1851 Great Exhibition Overseas Research Scholarship to the famous **Cavendish Laboratory** at Cambridge University. The director of the Cavendish was the renowned scientist Ernest Rutherford, who had investigated the nature of radioactive substances and had discovered the nucleus of the atom.

Rutherford asked Walton and another young researcher, John Cockcroft, to design and conduct an experiment to bombard the atomic nucleus with fast-moving tiny particles to find out if they could split it apart. This involved setting up a very high voltage system to speed up the particles and also some way of discovering whether or not the nucleus had been split.

Rutherford ran his laboratory on a shoestring budget and allowed Cockcroft and Walton only £500 to carry out this challenging project.

Meanwhile, American scientists and others were attempting to do the same thing with more powerful equipment and much more money. The race to split the atom was on. Two Swiss scientists were killed in the Alps, using the high voltages of lightning as their energy source.

To build the apparatus, Cockcroft and Walton used glass cylinders from old petrol pumps and lead from disused car batteries for insulation and protection. The high-voltage system accelerated protons, which struck a lithium target. If the energy of the proton was large enough it might penetrate the positively charged nucleus and break it apart.

On 14 April 1932 Walton observed flashes on the small fluorescent screen in the little hut at the base of the apparatus. He described it as follows: *'In the microscope there was a wonderful sight – lots of scintillations, looking just like stars flashing out momentarily on a clear dark night.'* Cockcroft and Rutherford confirmed that these

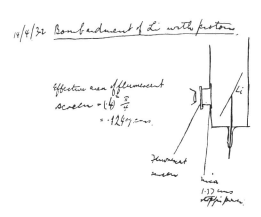

Part of a page from Walton's notebook on the day of the famous experiment

Ernest Walton

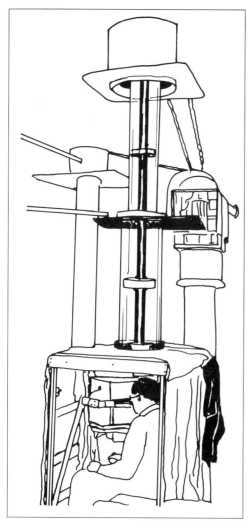

The Cockcroft–Walton accelerator
(Cavendish Laboratory, April 1932)

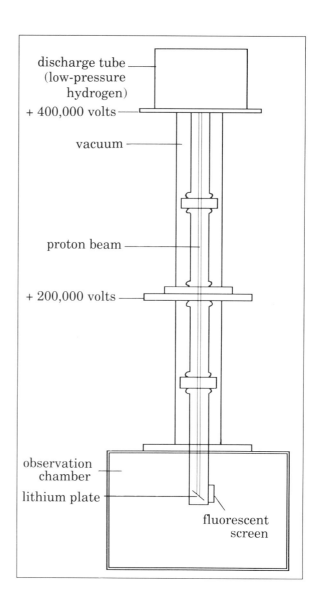

discharge tube
(low-pressure
hydrogen)

+ 400,000 volts

vacuum

proton beam

+ 200,000 volts

observation
chamber

lithium plate

fluorescent
screen

were indeed **alpha particles**, that is, two fragments of the lithium nucleus. The impossible had been achieved – the atom had been split into two (*atomos* in Greek means 'that which cannot be cut').

Walton and Cockcroft discovered that extra energy had been obtained and that this had come from the conversion of some of the mass of the nucleus into energy.

$$^{7}_{3}\text{Li} + ^{1}_{1}\text{p} \longrightarrow ^{4}_{2}\text{He} + ^{4}_{2}\text{He} + \text{energy}$$

Further calculations showed that for the first time Einstein's famous equation $E = mc^2$ had been proved experimentally.

These findings and the discovery of the **neutron** by Chadwick in the same year, also at the Cavendish, influenced the whole course of nuclear physics and heralded in the new age of atomic power.

In 1934 Ernest returned to Ireland and was appointed professor of physics at Trinity College Dublin. John Cockcroft became the director of the new Atomic Energy Authority, and received a knighthood. In 1951 they were both awarded the **Nobel Prize** for physics. Walton is the only Irish scientist to have been given this honour.

On 8 May 1992 Ernest Walton officially opened a new science and technology building, bearing his name, at Methodist College – a most fitting tribute by his old school.

A Methodist College pupil discussing her technology project with Professor Walton (right) and the Reverend Winston Good, President of the Methodist Church in Ireland

Plaque at the entrance to the Walton Science and Technology Building at Methodist College

12 Jocelyn Bell Burnell   1943–

Jocelyn Bell Burnell, 1992

Places of residence

Kilmore Road, Lurgan, County Armagh
  1943–56
Mount School, York 1956–61
Glasgow 1961–5
Cambridge 1965–8
Southampton 1968–73
Horsham, Surrey 1973–82
Edinburgh 1982–91
Milton Keynes 1991–

Family

Father   G. Philip Bell
Mother   M. Allison Kennedy
Married   Martin Burnell, 1968
Children One son

Susan Jocelyn Bell Burnell was born on 15 July 1943 in **Lurgan**, County Armagh. Her formal education began at the preparatory department attached to Lurgan College. Her parents believed strongly in the value of education and, indeed, her interest in astronomy can be traced back to the time when her father brought her home books on the subject from the Linen Hall Library in Belfast. Her father, a man of wide interests, was an architect and he was involved in designing new buildings for the Armagh Observatory; Jocelyn's interest in astronomy was further encouraged by the staff there.

Like many other able and intelligent people, Jocelyn failed her 11 plus selection examination – although she did sit it a year early. She entered Lurgan College where she showed a considerable talent for physics.

In 1956, when she was 13, Jocelyn was sent to the Mount School in York, a Quaker girls' boarding school. This school considered the study of science important, although it was lacking in suitable facilities and equipment. She was much influenced by her exceptional physics teacher, Mr Tillott.

Jocelyn did well in her exams and progressed to Glasgow University in 1961, where she was awarded a degree in physics. She was, in fact, the only young woman among the 50 students who sat final honours in natural philosophy (as physics was still called in Scottish universities).

During her university career Jocelyn took the opportunity of working as a summer student at the Jodrell Bank Observatory, since she hoped to do research in astronomy.

In 1965 Jocelyn applied for a post at the world-famous Cavendish Laboratory at Cambridge, and was accepted.

Her supervisor there was Dr Antony Hewish. These were the early days of the **space age**; manned satellites had been launched by the Russians and the Americans, and unmanned ones were being used for communications and weather forecasting. People were even talking about landing men on the moon.

Hewish designed and built a large **radio telescope**, which covered an area the size of two football pitches. There were over 2,000 copper aerials held up by long poles. Jocelyn spent her first two years at Cambridge helping to build this telescope.

Hewish and his team were trying to map the skies for some types of stars and galaxies that gave out radio waves as well as light. The signals received by the radio telescope were traced out on a chart recorder and Jocelyn's job was to analyse the charts – a tedious task, since every day they were 96 feet long!

On 28 November 1967 Jocelyn noticed a very regular pattern of pulses coming from a fixed point among the stars. The pulses had a precise time interval of just over 1.3 seconds. At first it was thought that these signals were man-made. Some people even suggested that they were sent by 'little green men' from outer space – so Dr Hewish and Jocelyn, with a touch of humour, called their project LGM 1.

They discovered that the signals came from a fixed place in the sky, moving around with the stars and returning to their original position four minutes earlier each evening. They ruled out the possibility that the signals were due to interference from cars or electrical appliances; other radio telescopes were picking up the signals, which meant that

Jocelyn Bell Burnell

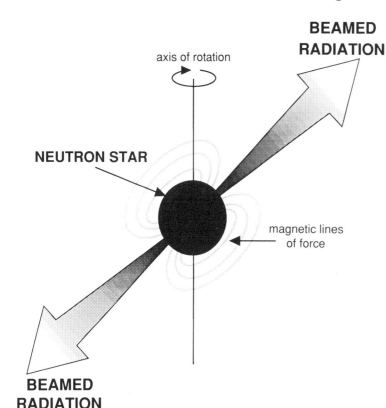

axis of rotation

BEAMED RADIATION

NEUTRON STAR

magnetic lines of force

BEAMED RADIATION

A pulsar

their own telescope was not faulty. Shortly afterwards more signals were received from three different parts of the sky, so they dismissed their 'little green men' theory.

In January 1968 Hewish, Jocelyn and three other research workers published a paper announcing the discovery of new radio sources – **pulsars** (short for **pulsa**ting **r**adio source).

This team proposed that a pulsar is a rotating neutron star with a powerful magnetic field, beaming out radio waves from its two poles like the lights of a lighthouse. A neutron star is one which has collapsed to a very small size (about 25 kilometres in diameter) under its own powerful gravity. A pinhead of matter from a neutron star would have a mass of 1,000,000 tonnes. Many pulsars have since been detected.

Jocelyn's original research completed, she left Cambridge to take up a Science Research Council fellowship at Southampton University, where she remained until 1973. She then joined the Mullard Space Science Laboratory in Dorking, Surrey, to study, using satellites and rockets, the X-rays emitted by heavenly bodies.

While working at Dorking Jocelyn learned that Dr Hewish had been awarded the **Nobel Prize** for physics for pioneering work on pulsars. Many people thought that although

Jocelyn Bell Burnell

Jocelyn had only been a research student, she should also have been awarded the prize, since it was by her persistence and dedication that the pulsars were discovered in the first place.

In 1982 Jocelyn joined the Royal Observatory in Edinburgh, where she eventually became head of the James Clerk Maxwell telescope section. This huge radio telescope, situated on top of a 14,000-foot volcanic mountain in Hawaii, is owned by the UK, Canada and the Netherlands in conjunction with the University of Hawaii.

In 1991 she was appointed professor of physics at the Open University, thus doubling the number of women physics professors in the UK!

Since her discovery of pulsars, Jocelyn has been awarded a number of prizes, including the Michelson Medal (Philadelphia), the Beatrice M. Tinsley Prize (American Astronomical Society) and the Herschel Medal from the Royal Astronomical Society. (Incidentally, since 1828 no woman had won this last prize; on that date the winner was Caroline Herschel, sister of William Herschel, the famous Astronomer-Royal.)

Jocelyn is aware of the many problems that beset women scientists, even today, including the assumption that if you marry, your career will come second to your husband's. She reckons that a woman scientist needs the support of her family, tremendous stamina, good organisational skills, and the sort of luck that enabled her to find the pulsars when she was looking for something else.

The Royal Observatory, Edinburgh

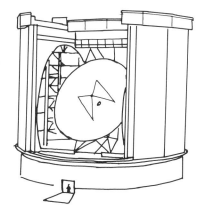

The James Clerk Maxwell radio telescope

49

SUGGESTIONS FOR FURTHER READING

We had of necessity to limit the amount of material that we could include on each scientist and inventor. If you would like to delve deeper into the lives of these interesting people, the following will help:

Alford, W.A.L. and J.W. Parkes. 'Sir James Murray, MD, a pioneer in the making of superphosphate', *Chemistry and Industry*, 15 August 1953, pp. 852–5

Bardon, Jonathan and Stephen Conlin. *Belfast: 1000 Years*, Blackstaff Press, Belfast, 1985

Corlett, John. *Aviation in Ulster*, Blackstaff Press, Belfast, 1981

Crowther, J.G. *Scientists of the Industrial Revolution*, Cresset Press, London, 1962

Fraser, Colin. *Harry Ferguson: Inventor and Pioneer*, John Murray, London, 1972

Harry, Owen G. 'The Hon. Mrs Ward and "A windfall for the microscope", of 1856 and 1864', *Annals of Science*, 41 (1984), pp. 471–82

Hartcup, Guy and T.E. Allibone. *Cockcroft and the Atom*, Adam Hilger, Bristol, 1984

Hayes, Maurice. *Sir Hans Sloane*, Hans Sloane Trustees, Belfast, 1987

Hendry, John. *Cambridge Physics in the Thirties*, Adam Hilger, Bristol, 1984

Hidden, A.E. and C.J. Latimer. *Science and Technology: Belfast and Its Region*, Institute of Irish Studies, Queen's University Belfast, 1987

Jewell, John. *Engineering for Life: The Story of Martin-Baker*, Martin-Baker Aircraft Company, Denham, 1979

Martin, Bill. *Harry Ferguson*, Ulster Folk and Transport Museum, Cultra, 1984

Mollan, Charles, William Davis and Brendan Finucane (eds). *Some People and Places in Irish Science and Technology*, Royal Irish Academy, Dublin, 1985

Mollan, Charles, William Davis and Brendan Finucane (eds). *Some More People and Places in Irish Science and Technology*, Royal Irish Academy, Dublin, 1991

Praeger, Robert Lloyd. *The Way That I Went*, Allen Figgis, Dublin, 1969

Smith, Crosbie and M. Norton Wise. *Energy and Empire: A Biographical Study of Lord Kelvin*, Cambridge University Press, 1991

Tait, P.G. *The Scientific Papers of Thomas Andrews*, Macmillan, London, 1889